# The Moki Snake Dance

BY WALTER HOUGH, PH. D.

With an introduction by
Joseph Traugott

*Avanyu Publishing Inc.*

Original material published by the Passenger
Department Santa Fe Route, 1898.
New material ©1992 by Avanyu Publishing Inc.

AVANYU PUBLISHING INC.
P.O. Box 27134
Albuquerque, NM 87125
(505)243-8485
(505)266-6128

Library of Congress Cataloging-in-Publication Data

Hough, Walter, 1859 - 1935.
    The Moki Snake dance / by Walter Hough;
with an introduction by Joseph Traugott.
        p.    cm.
ISBN 0-936755-19-9:    $5.95
    1. Snake dance. 2. Hopi Indians—Religion and
mythology. 3. Hopi Indians—Rites and ceremonies.
I. Title.
E99.H7H835 1992
299'.7—dc20                                        92-862
                                                    CIP

Front cover: "The Snake Dancers," an original watercolor
painting by Chad Burkhardt.
Typesetting and Layout by John Pella of Dynagraphics.
Photography by Focus Studio, Inc.
Back cover: "The Prayer at Dawn on the Morning of the Hopi
Snake Dance," by Eva Almond Withrow.

A T THE END of the nineteenth century, very few tourists had ever seen the Hopi Snake Dance. However many had heard tales of a dramatic ritual that only occurred every other year in isolated Indian villages in Arizona. This religious ceremony that Victorian society found so horrifying—and so fascinating—soon grew into a symbolic representation of "Indian Country" in the Southwest. The Passenger Department of the Santa Fe Railway played upon sensationalist, tourist visions of American Indians when it published Walter Hough's travel guide to *The Moki Snake Dance.*

The inscription on the title page describes Hough's text as "a popular account of that unparalleled dramatic pagan ceremony" with "incidental mention of their life and customs."[1] By starting with the narrative of the Snake Dance, this report focuses on one unusual aspect of the Hopi religion. Emphasizing this event subordinates the normal, day-to-day activities of Pueblo life on the Colorado Plateau. The concern for the unusual creates an artificial view of Pueblo life despite the accuracy of the information.

The tourist industry promoted this contradictory view of Southwestern Indians. On one hand the Hopi were

shown as a peaceful people who made elegant, hand-crafted objects. Educated travelers would consider these objects not as curios, but as works of art. But on the other hand the Snake Dance proved that these peoples were true "savages" at heart, in spite of their peaceful appearances. This duality captured the imaginations of elite visitors and provided a popular motivation for treks to the Southwest.

The combination of the "artistic" and the "savage" forged a mythic view of the Southwest and its inhabitants. Promoters of tourism have repeated this vision so often, and revived its form so successfully, that it persists today as a fresh illusion. Now this view has been sanitized into a sophisticated image called the "Santa Fe Style" or the "Southwestern Look."

*The Moki Snake Dance* incorporates many features from nineteenth century travel literature. Many popular literary periodicals including *Century Illustrated Monthly Magazine, Frank Leslie's Popular Monthly, Land of Sunshine,* and *The Cosmopolitan* featured articles describing travel to exotic lands. Often these were Oriental topics such as the "Fair Maids of Morocco,"[2] or "Tunisian Tints and Tones."[3] These kinds of essays highlight exotic subjects, strange customs, and sexual fantasy.

Southwestern essays played upon these themes. American travel subjects fit comfortably in this

"Orientalist" genre. Anthropologist Frank Cushing reported on tribal ways in "My Adventures in Zuni."[4] Cushing sketched daily life at Zuni Pueblo in New Mexico, his acceptance into the tribe, and his initiation in the Priesthood of the Bow. The details of Pueblo life presented tales that were totally alien to the educated readers of *Century Illustrated Monthly Magazine*.

By the mid-1890s the Southwest had developed into a popular travel subject in literary magazines. Charles Fletcher Lummis's sixteen-part essay "The Southwestern Wonderland"[5] presented a comprehensive view of the sights, peoples, crafts, and lifestyles of the traditional peoples of the Southwest. These kinds of articles developed the style, content, and illustrations which insured the popularity of *The Moki Snake Dance*.

These fantastic tales of the cultural "Other" often seemed more fiction than fact. The Santa Fe Railway validated *The Moki Snake Dance* in two ways. First the company used photographs rather than drawings to illustrate the travelogue. Second, the Railway authenticated the tale by employing an author with academic credentials who lent intellectual credibility to the text.

The sixty-six halftone illustrations reproduced photographs made by John K. Hillers, George Wharton James, Frederic Harmer Maude, and Adam Clark Vroman. Hillers, a noted documentary photographer, accompanied John Wesley Powell on his geological surveys between 1871 and 1879, and the Bureau of American Ethnology expeditions to the Southwest in the early 1880s. James and Maude were partners in a commercial photography business in Pasadena, California; James went on to publish a series of Western travelogues illustrated with his photographs. Vroman made the most sensitive images of the Southwest during this period, but had to sell books and photographic supplies to make a living.

Historians often dismiss these photographers as makers of ethnographic or tourist images. However, contemporary aesthetic assessments of Hillers's and Vroman's work interpret their photographs as art, as well as ethnography. Both made large format glass plate negatives which they printed directly without enlargement or reduction. Their images exhibit a sensitivity to their subjects which captures the subtleties of life in the Pueblos within a Victorian aesthetic.

Vroman's work found its way into a variety of turn-of-the-century publications and served to refute racist assessments of Indian life. Often publishers vignetted halftone illustrations of these photographs. The vignettes imitated the look of the more elite, handmade wood engravings. Lummis used Vroman's photographs to illustrate numerous articles about Native Americans in *Land of Sunshine* and *Out West* magazines. After the publication of Vroman's images in *The Moki Snake Dance*, the Santa Fe Railway again used his images for a similar publication called *Indians of the Southwest*. George A. Dorsey, curator of Anthropology at the Field Columbian Museum in Chicago, wrote this 1903 guide to the sights along the railway.

John L. Stoddard illustrated his 1904 travelogue of the Grand Canyon[6] with reproductions of Vroman's photographs. However, Stoddard does not credit Vroman as the source of the images. Burton Holmes illustrated his 1904 travelogue on "Moki Land"[7] with photographs by Vroman and Sumner Matteson. Vroman's photographs were so popular by the first decade of the twentieth century that fifty-three of his images graced a set of playing cards sold by the Fred Harvey Company along the Santa Fe Railway.

The Detroit Publishing Company offered the ultimate promotion of Vroman's imagery. The famous expeditionary photographer William Henry Jackson founded this company to promote photographic visions of the West. The Detroit Publishing Company sold both hand-colored enlargements and "Phototints" of Vroman's black-and-white images.

Phototints look like modern color photographs. Unlike hand-colored images, Phototints have no mark of the artist's hand. They look extremely naturalistic because the process used photographic negatives to print multiple colors through a callographic technique.

Detroit Publishing Company bought the rights to this process from a Swiss firm which had patented the process.

Jackson marketed the results of the improved process under the trade name Phototint. Their photographic accuracy must have seemed larger than life to Victorian audiences accustomed to clumsily hand-colored images. The popularity of illustrated, literary travelogues of the Southwest must have encouraged a lively trade in the Detroit Publishing Company's color images.

The well-educated audiences who read nineteenth-century travelogues often dismissed tales such as the Snake Dance as fiction. Publishers employed authority figures to lend credibility and respectability to stories which seemed fanciful. Anthropologist Hough solved this problem of credibility for the Santa Fe Railway.

Hough grew up in West Virginia and studied natural science at West Virginia University. Later he accepted a position in the Department of Ethnography at the National Museum in Washington, D.C. In 1894 he finished his Ph.D. in anthropology and continued working at the Smithsonian Institution in Washington, D.C. Hough assisted Dr. Jesse Walter Fewkes during his 1896 excavation in the area surrounding the Hopi villages. This combination of formal anthropological training, employment by a respected museological institution, and first-hand observation provided *The Moki Snake Dance* with intellectual credibility. Ironically the publication only lists Hough's academic credentials.

Hough observed the 1897 Snake Dance at the village of Walpi. However, as an outsider, he was not privy to the secret ceremonies that occurred in the religious rooms called kivas. Hough substituted descriptions of this secret information that his colleague Fewkes had published in the *Journal of American Ethnology and Archaeology.* Fewkes presents an authoritative image in print. However there is some question whether this material was really Fewkes's research.

Fewkes observed the Snake Ceremonies at First Mesa in 1891 and 1893 with Alexander M. Stephen. Stephen had been living at First Mesa after coming to Hopi in 1881. He learned the Hopi language and studied local lifeways. The Hopi liked Stephen and in 1892 initiated him into the Snake Society at the village of Shipaulovi. Stephen kept a journal of ethnographic information beginning in the late 1800s until his untimely death in the spring of 1894.

Elsie Clews Parsons, who edited Stephen's journals, states that Fewkes had used Stephen's notes from 1891 and 1893 which were "run together and published by Fewkes."[8] Anthropologists Fewkes and Hough

each published accounts of the Hopi Snake Dance.[9] However Stephen, who lacked formal training as an anthropologist, assembled the most accurate ethnographic record of the snake rituals and Hopi life. The anthropologists appropriated Stephen's data, but did not adequately credit him as the source of their information.

In spite of the sensationalism of Hough's narrative, *The Moki Snake Dance* is important because it is one of the first tourist publications to present Indians as worthy of serious study and investigation. On the surface *The Moki Snake Dance* appears to be a simple travelogue and an ethnographic account. However, it is much more complex than a simple ethnography. Hough also presents an unconscious, revealing view of anthropology, photographic art, and tourist visions of Native Americans at the end of the nineteenth century.

Joseph Traugott
Curator, Jonson Gallery
University of New Mexico

Endnotes

1 Walter Hough. *The Moki Snake Dance*. Chicago: Passenger Department of the Santa Fe Railway, 1898, title page.

2 Frederick A. Ober. "Fair Maids of Morocco," *Frank Leslie's Popular Monthly*. Vol. XLII (1897), No. 5., pp.491-498.

3 Henry Haynie. "Tunisian Tints and Tones," *The Cosmopolitan*. Vol. XVII (1894), No. 6., pp.670-685.

4 Frank Cushing. "My Adventures in Zuni," *Century Illustrated Monthly Magazine*. Vol. 25 (1892), pp. 191-207, 500-511, and Vol. . 26 (1883), pp. 28-43.

5 Charles Fletcher Lummis. "The Southwestern Wonderland." *Land of Sunshine*. Vol. 4, No. 5 (April, 1896) through Vol. 6, No. 2 (July, 1897).

6 John L. Stoddard. "The Grand Canyon of the Colorado," in *John L. Stoddard's Lectures*, Volume X. Boston: Balch Brothers Co., l904.

7 Burton Holmes. *The Burton Holmes Lectures*, Volume Six. New York: McClure Philips & Co., l905.

8 Alexander M. Stephen, *Hopi Journal of Alexander M. Stephen*, edited by Elsie Clews Parsons. New York: Columbia University Press, 1936, p. 579.

9 Fewkes' accounts have been compiled and reprinted as *Hopi Snake Ceremonies*. Albuquerque: Avanyu Publishing Inc., 1985.

# THE MOKI
## SNAKE DANCE

# The Moki Snake Dance

☞

*A popular account of that unparalleled
dramatic pagan ceremony of the
Pueblo Indians of Tusayan,
Arizona, with incidental
mention of their life
and customs.*

☞

BY WALTER HOUGH, PH. D.

*Sixty-four Half-tone Illustrations from
Special Photographs.*

FORTY-SECOND THOUSAND.

Published by Passenger Department
THE SANTA FE.
1901

DANCE ROCK, WOLPI.

RACER.

JUST at the dawn of an August morning groups of eager watchers sit along the precipitous cliffs or slopes of a mesa bearing on its crest a Moki village. All faces are turned in one direction; the gray light becomes many-hued before the near approach of the sun. A murmur passes through the crowd; in the distance a number of dark forms are seen running toward the mesa; nearer they come, pursued by boys and girls with wands of cornstalk, and run up the tortuous trail as though on level ground. As the sun appears above the eastern horizon the winner passes over the roof of the Snake *kiva* and the day of the Snake dance has begun with the Snake race. The runners deposit the melon vines, corn and other products they have carried from the fields, and the panting victor gets for his prize the glory of winning. As in the Greek games, the Mokis honor the swift runner.

As the day wears on the interest centers in the *kivas*, where swarthy priests are bringing to a close the mysterious rites begun days before, when the astronomer Sun priest had directed the town crier to announce the commencement of the ceremony. Since that time the priests had descended into the *kiva*, and a fleet runner had each day carried plumed prayer-sticks to the distant springs and shrines. Four days to the north, west, south and east snakes had been hunted. Then came the Antelope dance on the evening before the Snake dance; the sixteen songs and drama were enacted in the *kiva* while the

3

WOLPI, "THE PLACE OF THE GAP."

Snake race was being run, and the time
is now ripe for the final spectacle. The
snakes have been washed and placed in jars and
the costuming begins. Long-haired, painted priests in
scanty attire emerge from the *kivas* and go on various
errands. Visitors and Mokis examine one another with
mutual curiosity; the children are having a jolly time,
for the Snake dance comes in their village but once in
two years, and white visitors are sure to bring candy to
put a climax to the stuffing of new corn, melons and
other good things of August.

Other dances of the Mokis are more pleasing, as the
Kachina dances, with their mirth and music, or the
Flute dance, full of color and ceremony, but the Snake
dance attracts with a potent fascination. One gets so
interested in the progress of the dance that the antici-
pated element of horror does not appear amid the
rhythmic movement and tragic gestures of the dancers
with here and there the sinuous undulation of a venomous rattlesnake. Along the sky-line of the houses and
on every available foothold and standing place are spectators. At Wolpi, the top of the mushroom-shaped
rock is a favorite seat. The crowd is hardly less interesting than the dancers. Everyone, except the white
visitor, is in gala costume, Moki and Navajo vying in
gaudy colors. The Moki maidens have their hair done

4

up in great whorls of shining blackness at the sides of
their heads. The women, who have brushed away the
evidences of preparation for the feast to follow the dance,
now appear at their best, and the children dash around,
consuming unlimited slices of watermelon. Mormons,
be-pistoled cowboys, prospectors, army officers, teachers
from the schools, scientists, photographers, and tourists
in the modern costume suitable for camp life, mingle
with the Indian spectators in motley confusion. Not
less than one hundred white people witnessed the Snake
dance at Wolpi in 1897. Each year there is a larger
attendance.

If the visitor will look around he will see that at one
side of the dance plaza there is a bower of green cottonwood branches, the *kisi*, where the snakes are to be kept
in readiness during the dance. The descending sun
casts a long shadow eastward from the *kisi* when a priest
enters the plaza with a bag containing the reptiles and
quickly disappears
among the branches.
This is the man who
hands the snakes

MOKI CHILDREN.

out to the
dancers
through a
small open-
ing in the

ANTELOPE PRIEST.

front of the *kisi*. The expectancy now is intense. All eyes are fixed in the direction from which the priests will appear. The sun sinks lower and the evening colors steal into the landscape, but no one notices them.

"Here they come!" The grand entry of the Antelope priests causes a sensation. With bare feet, and their semi-nude bodies streaked with white paint; a band of white on the chin from mouth to ear, rattles of tortoise shell tied to the knee, embroidered kilts of white cotton fastened around the loins, necklaces of shell and turquoise, and fox skins hanging behind from the belt, these priests present a startling though not unattractive appearance. At the head of the file comes the Antelope Chief bearing his *tiponi* or sacred badge across his left arm. Next comes the bearer of the medicine bowl. All the other priests carry a small rattle in either hand. With stately mien, and looking to neither right nor left, the Antelope priests pass four times around the plaza to the left, each sprinkling sacred meal and stamping violently upon the plank in the ground in front of the *kisi*. The hole in the middle of the plank is the opening into the under-world and the dancers stamp upon it to inform the spirits of their ancestors that a ceremony is in progress. Fortunate is the man who breaks the board with his foot! When the circuit is made, the Antelope priests line up in front of the *kisi* facing outward; there is a hush and the Snake priests enter.

6

The grand entry of the Snake priests is dramatic to the last degree. With majestic strides they hasten into the plaza, every attitude full of energy and fierce determined purpose. The costume of the priests of the sister society of Antelopes is gay in comparison with that of the Snake priests. Their bodies rubbed with red paint, their chins blackened and outlined with a white stripe, their dark red kilts and moccasins, their barbaric ornaments, give the Snake priests a most somber and diabolical appearance. Around the plaza, by a wider circuit than the Antelopes, they go striking the *sipapu* plank with the foot and fiercely leaping upon it with wild gestures. Four times the circuit is made; then a line is formed facing the line of the Antelopes, who cease shaking their rattles which simulate the warning note of the rattlesnake. A moment's pause and the rattles begin again and a deep humming chant accompanies them. The priests sway from side

FLUTE DANCE, ORAIBI.    *Higgins, photo*

to side, sweeping their eagle-feather snake whips toward
the ground ; the song grows louder and the lines sway
backward and forward toward each other like two long,
undulating serpents. The bearer of the medicine walks
back and forth between the lines and sprinkles the
charm liquid to the compass points.

All at once the Snake line breaks up into groups of
three, composed of the "carrier" and two attendants.
The song becomes more animated and the groups dance
or rather hop, around in a circle in front of the *kisi*, one
attendant (the "hugger") placing his arm over the
shoulder of the "carrier" and the other (the "gatherer")
walking behind. In all this stir and excitement it has
been rather difficult to see why the "carrier" dropped on
his knees in front of the *kisi ;* a moment later he is seen
to rise with a squirming snake, which he places midway
in his mouth, and the trio dance around the circle, followed by other trios bearing hideous snakes. The
"hugger" waves his feather wand before the snake to
attract its attention, but the reptile inquiringly thrusts

SPECTATORS, WOLPI.

its head against the
"carrier's" breast and
cheeks and twists its
body into knots and
coils. On come the
demoniacal groups, to
music now deep and
resonant and now ris-
ing to a frenzied pitch,
accompanied by the un-
ceasing sibilant rattles
of the Antelope chorus.
Four times around and
the "carrier" opens
his mouth and drops
the snake to the ground

KACHINA DANCERS.

and the "gatherer" dextrously picks it up, adding in the same manner from time to time other snakes, till he may have quite a bundle composed of rattlesnakes, bull snakes and arrow snakes. The bull snakes are large and showy, and impressive out of proportion to their harmfulness. When all the snakes have been duly danced around the ring, and the nerve tension is at its highest pitch, there is a pause; the old priest advances to an open place and sprinkles sacred meal on the ground, outlining a ring with the six compass points, while the Snake priests gather around. At a given signal the snakes are thrown on the meal drawing' and a wild scramble for them ensues, amid a rain of spittle from the spectators on the walls above. Only an instant and the priests start up, each with one or more snakes; away they dart for the trail to carry the rain-bringing messengers to their native hiding places. They dash down the mesa and reappear far out on the trails below, running like the wind with their grewsome burdens. The Antelope priests next march gravely around the plaza four times, thumping the sunken plank, and file out to their *kiva*. The ceremony is done.

Stay! there is another scene in this drama which may seem a fitting

9

NAVAJO SPECTATOR.

termination. Whoever wishes may go to look on, but not everyone goes. The Snake priests return, go to the *kiva* and remove all their trappings, come out to the edge of the cliff where the medicine women have brought great bowls of a dark liquid brewed in secrecy and mystery. No one knows the herbs and spells in this liquid but Salako of Wolpi, the head Snake woman of the Moki pueblos. The priests drink of the medicine; in about forty-five seconds it sees the light of day again. They repeat the operation, and so goes on a scene that beggars description. Even scientific equanimity cannot observe without qualms that this is a purification ceremony, carried out by the priests with the ruthlessness of devotion. This feature of the dance, however, will never become popular. Various explanations of the purpose of the medicine have been current. It has been supposed, among others, to be the antidote for the venom of the rattlesnake. Probably it is only for ceremonial purification; at any rate it is a good preparation for the great feast following the dance.

For this feast fair maidens and trim women come bearing trays of gala bread, well cooked meat, corn pudding and other dainties and substantials in profusion. That night there is feasting and every Moki gets what the cowboys call a "mortal gorge." Next day and the day following the boys and girls have great sport in the pueblos. A young man will take a ribbon, a piece of

DANCE ROCK AND KISI.

MOKI GIRLS.

*Hillers, photo.*

11

Copyright, 1896, by G. Wharton James.                    Used by permission.

ANTELOPE CIRCUIT, ORAIBI.

pottery or any other object and appear on the house-
tops or street, only to be set upon and chased by the
girls bent on securing the prize.

Many questions suggest themselves to everyone who
witnesses the Snake dance. Some do not seem to be
very easy to answer, and some are those which, perhaps,
the wisest and most lore-learned priest cannot answer
now after the lapse of centuries since
the ceremony began. Still, most of us
can leave them for the scientists to pore over.
What everyone wants
to know

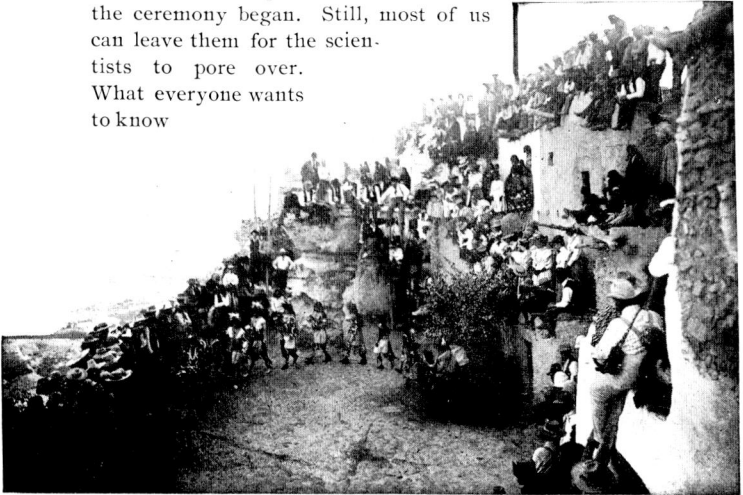

CIRCUIT OF ANTELOPE PRIESTS, WOLPI.            *Vroman, photo.*

is whether the snakes are drugged or have their fangs
removed, and, if not, whether they ever bite their captors.
Men who have attended as many as ten dances in various
Moki pueblos say that they have never seen a dancer
bitten by a poisonous snake, while others have seen a
reptile strike or perhaps fasten upon the hand of a
dancer and require to be shaken off. In the present
state of the question everyone must judge for himself.
One thing is very certain, the Mokis are extremely care-
ful with a poisonous snake. At Wolpi, in 1897, two

ENTRANCE OF SNAKE PRIESTS, WOLPI.

*Vroman, photo.*

large rattlesnakes, which from their age had perhaps
been danced around the ring before, coiled together and
for a time refused to move, almost breaking up the performance. An experienced snake driver at length suc-
ceeded in making them uncoil, when they were easily
picked up. This is thought to be the secret of handling
the rattlesnake ; never to handle him when he is coiled,
for it is said that this serpent cannot strike without

coiling. Then, too, the snakes may have been somewhat subjugated by their bewildering treatment, since
they were dragged from their haunts by naked men
armed with hoes and sticks, thrust with other snakes
into a bag and brought to the *kivas*, and afterward
washed and uncivilly flung about.

The Snake dance is exciting enough, but the two or
three men who have witnessed the sinister rites called
"snake washing" in the dark *kiva* tell a story which
makes the blood curdle. Doctor Fewkes relates this
experience as follows:

"The Snake priests, who stood by the snake jars which were
in the east corner of the room, began to take out the reptiles, and
stood holding several of them in their hands behind Su-pe-la, so
that my attention was distracted by them. Su-pe-la then
prayed, and after a short interval two rattlesnakes were
handed him, after which other venomous snakes were
passed to the others,
and each of the six
priests who sat around
the bowl held two rat-
tlesnakes by the necks
with their heads ele-
vated above the bowl.
A low noise from the
rattles of the priests,

*Vroman, photo.*

CIRCUIT OF SNAKE PRIESTS, WOLPI.

ANTELOPES IN LINE, ORAIBI.

which shortly after was accompanied by a melodious hum by
all present, then began. The priests who held the snakes beat
time up and down above the liquid with the reptiles, which,
although not vicious, wound their bodies around the arms of the
holders. The song went on and frequently changed, growing
louder and wilder, until it burst forth into a fierce, blood-cur-
dling yell, or war-cry. At this moment the heads of the snakes
were thrust several times into the liquid, so that even parts
of their bodies were submerged, and were then drawn out,
not having left the hands of the priests, and forcibly thrown
across the room upon the sand mosaic, knocking down the
crooks and other objects placed about it. As they fell on the sand
picture three Snake priests stood in readiness, and while the reptiles squirmed about or coiled for defense, these men with their
snake whips brushed them back and forth in the sand of the altar.
The excitement which accompanied this ceremony cannot be
adequately described. The low song, breaking into piercing
shrieks, the red-stained singers, the snakes thrown by the chiefs,
and the fierce attitudes of the reptiles as they landed on the sand
mosaic, made it next to impossible to sit calmly down and quietly

LINE-UP BEFORE KISI, WOLPI.

note the events which followed one after another in quick succession. The sight haunted me for weeks afterwards, and I can never forget this wildest of all the aboriginal rites of this strange people, which showed no element of our present civilization. It was a performance which might have been expected in the heart of Africa rather than in the American Union, and certainly one could not realize that he was in the United States at the end of the nineteenth century. The low weird song continued while other rattlesnakes were taken in the hands of the priests, and as the song rose again to the wild war-cry, these snakes were also plunged into the liquid and thrown upon the writhing mass which now occupied the place of the altar. Again and again this was repeated until all the snakes had been treated in the same way, and reptiles, fetiches, crooks and sand were mixed together in one confused mass. As the excitement subsided and the snakes crawled to the corners of the *kiva*, seeking vainly for protection, they were again pushed back in the mass, and brushed together in the sand in order that their

16

bodies might be thoroughly dried. Every snake in the collection was thus washed, the harmless varieties being bathed after the venomous. In the destruction of the altar by the reptiles the snake *ti-po-ni* stood upright until all had been washed, and then one of the priests turned it on its side, as a sign that the observance had ended. The low, weird song of the Snake men continued, and gradually died away until there was no sound but the warning rattle of the snakes, mingled with that of the rattles in the hands of the chiefs, and finally the motion of the snake whips ceased, and all was silent."*

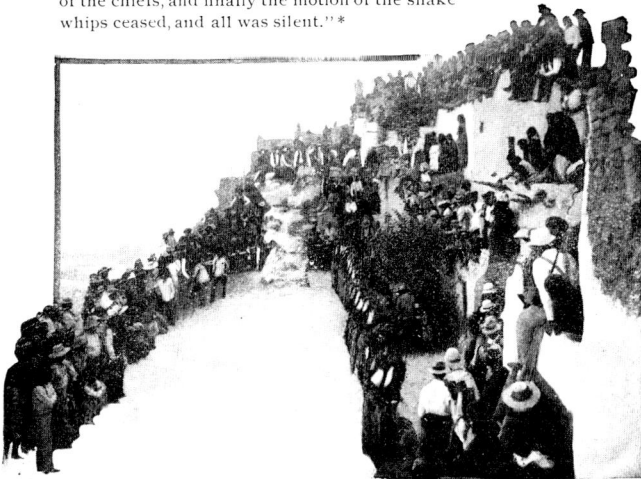

CHANTING BEFORE KISI, WOLPI. *Vroman, photo.*

The Mokis have an antidote for snake bite made from the root of a plant called by botanists *Gaura parviflora*. They do not know the white man's fiery antidote and panacea, but expert opinion declares that one remedy is as good as the other. Snakes are scarce in Tusayan, although they seem plentiful at the Snake dances. Still,

*The Snake Ceremony at Wolpi, Jour. Am. Eth. & Arch., Vol. IV, pp. 84, 85.

FACE VIEW, SNAKE PRIESTS, ORAIBI.

it requires four days of vigilant search to the four points of the compass to procure enough. Some years ago, a Wolpi farmer, while in his cornfield, was bitten on the hand by a rattlesnake, and the combined efforts of the Indian doctors and some white people who happened to be near by were applied for his relief. After a great deal of suffering he recovered. Soon after, the Snake Society informed him that he must become a Snake priest, because he was favored by the rattlesnake. Perhaps Intiwa, for that was his name, did

CHANTING BEFORE KISI, ORAIBI.

Maude, photo.

TRIO OF DANCERS.

not see where the favor came in, but he was duly installed as a member of the Society.

Turning now from this strange, nerve-wrenching scene, which many have crossed the mysterious Painted Desert north of the Little Colorado river to witness, some general account of the Mokis should be interesting. Perched upon high, warm-tinted sandstone mesas, narrow like the decks of great Atlantic liners, are their clustered dwellings, scarcely to be distinguished from the living rock upon which they rest. High up above the plain, viewing from all sides an almost illimitable distance, basking in the brilliant sunshine from sunrise to sunset, bathed in the pure, life-giving air, the Mokis, or "good people," * as they delight to call themselves, must feel freedom in its truest sense. Here is isolation. In the long centuries the Mokis have dwelt here they have had few visitors. The all-venturing Spaniards, in their sixteenth century quest for the mythical doorposts of gold set with jewels, were way-weary long before their toilsome journey brought them to the base of the giant mesas. In this semi-desert, far out of the trail traveled by friends and foes, the Mokis found the desired

* The name by which these people are known among themselves is *Hopi*, whose signification is as stated. *Moki* is a derisive name, originally applied by outsiders, which unfortunately seems fated to stick.

19

DANCERS, ORAIBI.

seclusion and peace after the harrying of the Apache
and Ute, whose hand was against every man.

Perhaps the word mysterious as applied to the desert
may need explanation to city-dwellers and those who are
accustomed to limited horizons. In the desert a new sensation comes to those who have exhausted the repertory of
sensations at the end of a rapid century. In the desert
the desert is supreme. The sense of freedom and exhil-
aration, which everyone must feel, is personal ; the desert is titanic ; gradually it com-
pels awe and wonder. A feeling

Copyright, 1896, by F. H. Maude.
THE DANCE, ORAIBI.

Used by permission.

of vastness, almost infinity, dawns in the mind with
an impression of mystery. Here thousands of square
miles stretch in iridescent beauty to the violet horizon
or to the velvety blue mountains; nearer stand the
strange forms of the volcanic buttes ; across the sand
plain the purple cloud shadows float, attended by
the tawny sand whirlwinds ; a distant thunderstorm
marches along, dwarfed in all its energy to a small part
of the scene. The morning and evening reveal new

20

coloring and beauty beyond the power of pen or pencil
to depict. With the night new experiences come in the
desert. In the clear air of Tusayan myriads of stars are
revealed. It is not often the good fortune of the astronomer to enjoy such skies for observation. Stars of low
magnitude, rarely seen elsewhere, are easily found in
the night heavens of Tusayan. It may seem like
romancing, but it is true, the powdery, misty starlight
is strong enough to admit of reading the dial of a watch
and to distinguish the outline of mesas and buttes miles
away. Then the silence of the night is overpowering.
Not a cricket chirps and no animal disturbs the almost
oppressive silence.

When the *conquistadores* came to Tusayan, some
three hundred and fifty years ago, they found the Mokis
high up on the mesas, but not on the rocky tops where
the towns are now built. This meeting of the Conquerors

THE DANCE, WOLPI.          *Vroman, photo.*

FOOD BRINGING. *Voth, photo.*

and the Mokis has always seemed a picturesque subject. The Spaniards recorded their experiences and the Mokis relate the traditions of the experiences of their forefathers passed along by word of mouth, accurate as if written down. Beneath the town then perched on the higher slope of the Wolpi mesa, came a band of horsemen, some clad in armor and warlike trappings badly damaged and battered by wear and tear, but impressive to the Indian, who for the first time saw the white man. Perhaps the Mokis were not very friendly. The warrior priest strode down the trail followed by his band and drew a line of sacred meal across the path to the town, over which, according to immemorial custom, no one might come with impunity. This "dead line" brought death instead to the Mokis. At the fire of the dreadful guns they fled up the narrow trail to refuge. The Spaniards dared not follow up the rocky way, but camped for the night by a spring. In the morning the timorous Mokis came down with presents of food and woven stuffs. This is the first picture of the Mokis of Wolpi, who were thus introduced to the proud Castilian, bent on reaching new lands to despoil. Later came a new company, bringing priests to turn the peaceful people from their native superstitions. When the town of Wolpi burst upon their view it was a new town, built on the highest summit of the mesa ! The timid people had moved up from the lower point, taking with them house beams, stones, and every other portion of their dwellings. The trails were rendered inaccessible and the

22

people ascended and descended by a movable ladder. Still they received the priests and submitted to the enforced labor of building a church, carrying, with infinite toil, beams of cottonwood from the Little Colorado. Many of these carved beams now support the roofs of the pagan *kivas*. Later, when the oppression grew too great, the Mokis committed one of the few overt acts which may be charged against them. They threw the "long gowns," as they called the friars, over the cliffs, and cut loose once for all from the foreign religion. This ended the contact of the whites with the Mokis for long years until, at last, the Government took them under its protection.

But the Moki had immemorial enemies, as has been hinted. The Apache, who centuries ago came out of the high north, a rude and fierce being, incapable of high things, is responsible for the acropolis towns all along the trails by which the Moki clans came to Tusayan. The history of the wanderings of the Moki to this land of scant promise would be interesting if all the threads

*Used by permission.*

SNAKES, IN KIVA.

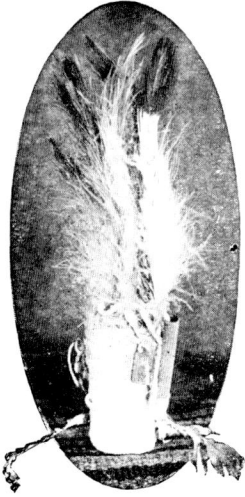

TIPONI.

could be gathered together. The story goes somewhat in this fashion : Long ago — how long one may guess as well as another and get as near to it as the Mokis, who say it was "very, very when"— groups of Indians belonging to the great Uto-Aztecan stock and other pueblo stocks lived over all this region. The limits of this vast region are more accurately found in the States of Utah, Colorado, New Mexico and Arizona and reach over into Mexico. This ruin-strewn expanse tells the story of many wanderings and movings about, through the forgotten years, before the pueblo peoples were settled in the places where the white man found them. The re-mains of ancient monarchies are, per-haps, more interesting from their connection with the world's history, but there is a fascination also in the leveled cities of the Southwest, under which lie the rude records of the ancients of the New World. In the course of time and through various vicissitudes of war, famine or disease, some of these groups were broken up and the survivors forced to seek refuge in other tribes of their kin. This has been going on for millenniums. The organization of these tribes was rather loose, and consisted of clans which are made up of those related by blood ; marriages were, as they are now, prohibited between members of the same clan. This was another cause of mixture. So it happened that in our deserts there was a wandering of the ancient people like that of the chosen people, but their simple clothing waxed old, their towns waxed old, and their mother corn only blessed them by hard labor. It would seem at the first glance that some great unrest filled the

24

WOLPI, FROM BELOW.

*Hillers, photo.*

breasts of the ancient pueblo dwellers and forced them
to forever move on. Ruins without number attest the
flux of population over an area in which the countries
of the ancients of the Old World would be lost. Still
these ruins are not without order; the clans moved
along together in those dark ages, so that the ruins are
found in groups. Thus if we hark back on the trail by
which some of the clans came from the south to Tusayan, the Mogollon Mountains at Chavez Pass will show

TWIN BUTTES AND CLOUDS.

*Vroman, photo.*

AN ARIZONA CLOUD EFFECT. *Vroman, photo.*

two large ruins to which Moki tradition gives the name
of "the place of the antelopes." Thirty-two miles to
the north is the next stopping place, and the clans must
have prospered in the valley of the Little Colorado at
Winslow, for here are the ruins of five towns, called by
those versed in the lore of the past Homolobi, or "the
place of the two views." The grand panorama of the
Moki buttes seen from "the place of the antelopes"
was still visible from Homolobi, though at a lower view-
point. Long before the *conquistadores* came to ravage
the New World, the people of Homolobi had abandoned
their towns and taken up their weary journey to Tusayan, where now are seven towns of the "good people."
It is interesting to find that in Wolpi different clans live
in different sections of the town just as they had camped
together in the old days, and in the order in which they
came from their desert wandering. This journey of
some of the clans of Mokis began much farther away
than the two faint points on the dim Mogollones where
antelopes range to this day. To say that the Mokis
belong by language to the great Uto-Aztecan stock
means that in bygone times they were in contact with
the Aztecs or may even have been a branch of that far-
famed people. Just here, if it might be possible to correct

26

AN ARIZONA CAMP.

the popular hallucination in reference to the Aztecs,
it would be well to say that that mysterious and ever-
vanishing people were nothing more nor less than American Indians. In some lines of work the Mokis of
Homolobi, for instance, were superior to the Aztecs.
Romance and the Aztecs have been sadly mixed up by
the writers of a past generation.

The towns of Tusayan are seven. Wolpi, "the place
of the gap," named for the deep cut across the mesa on
which it is built, is best known. The people are very
friendly and are more advanced than the other tribes.

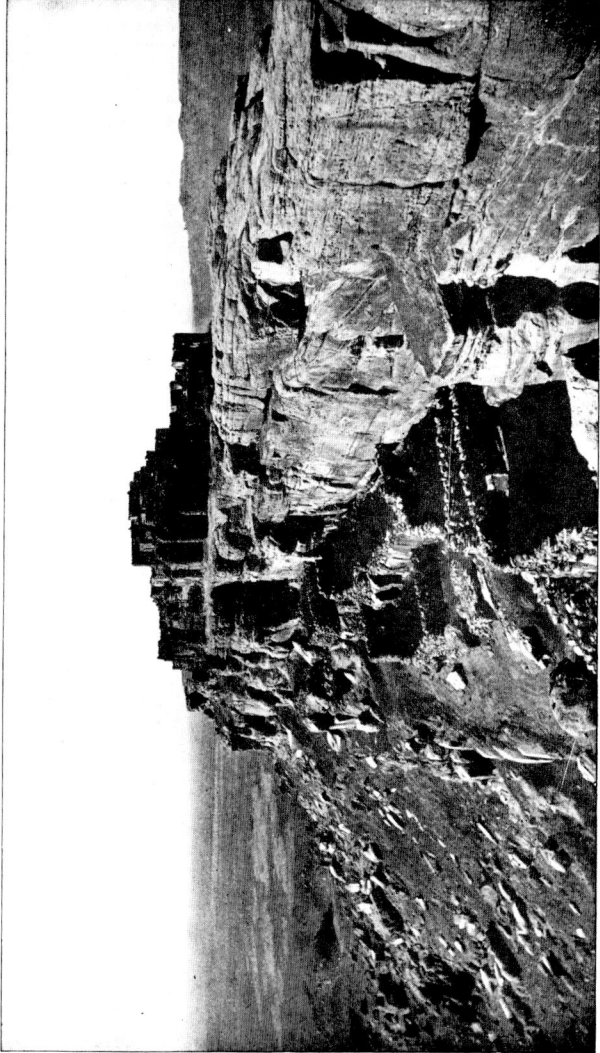

PUEBLO OF WOLPI.

*Hillers photo.*

There is a school and many families live below the mesa in red-roofed houses. Perhaps in a few years the old pueblo will be abandoned and the quaint customs forgotten.

Next to Wolpi on the east is Si-chom'-ovi, "the mound of flowers," an offshoot of Wolpi — on account of a disagreement, it is thought.

Ha'-no (also known as Te'-wa) is the third village on the First or East Mesa, near the gap. Hano is a village of Tewans who were induced to come from the Rio Grande two centuries ago to assist in defending the peaceful Mokis from the Apaches and Utes. They were located at the head of the easiest trail up the mesa, and on a smooth rock face is an inscription recording a battle in which they vanquished the Utes. These "keepers of the trail" are expert potters, and most of the Moki ware is of their handicraft. It seems strange to find in Tusayan these foreigners still speaking a language different from that of their neighbors.

Seven miles to the west, across the valley from Wolpi, the point of Second or Middle Mesa stands out in silhouette. The first town is called Mi-shong'-movi, second in size in Tusayan. The Snake dance is held here in odd years, as at Wolpi. At such times the large interior plaza is extremely picturesque. On

WOLPI FOOT TRAIL.    *Hillers, photo.*

PUEBLO OF SICHOMOVI.

*Hillers, photo.*

PUEBLO OF TEWA (HANO).

*Hillers, photo.*

the east trail to Mishonginovi there is a curious
hanging rock forming an
arch under which the trail
passes.

CORN CARRIER.

Back of Mishonginovi is
the small town of Shi-paul'-ovi, " the
place of the peaches," the most picturesquely located of the Moki pueblos, and with the most elevated
situation. Shipaulovi is a comparatively modern town,
having been formed by families from Shung o'-pavi since
the Spaniards introduced peaches. Here the Snake
dance is held in even years, alternating with that of the
Flute.

Shungopavi, " the place of the reed grass," is a few
miles west of Shipaulovi. Reed grass is prescribed for
the mats wound around the ceremonial wedding blankets
of white cotton. A small country place of Shungopavi
is located at Little Burro Spring,
some twelve miles south of the
town.

Oraibi, with its fifty mile distant
little offshoot, Mo''-en-kop'-i, marks
the extreme western, as Taos marks
the eastern, extent of the pueblo
region. Nearly one-half, or about
eight hundred, of the Mokis live in
Oraibi. The Snake Society at this
pueblo, though fewer in numbers
than at several of the other towns,
gives an interesting performance.
The large open plaza where the dance
is held offers excellent opportunities
for photographing and for viewing
the spectacle.

MAIL CARRIER.

31

SPINNER.

In the even years visitors to Tusayan may see three Snake dances — those of Oraibi, Shipaulovi, and Shungopavi, unless the dates coincide, which they are unlikely to do. The Province of Tusayan, where the Mokis now live and thrive, is not a total desert waste, although the first impression of those accustomed to green fields and frequent rains is likely to be to the contrary. Drought-defying plants bloom at certain seasons, and fill wide stretches with color. Along the sandy washes, adjacent to the pueblos, which rarely by the good will of the rain gods show a silver glint of water, are corn fields and melon and bean patches, well cared for and jealously guarded by their owners. Internecine war is waged against the freebooting crows, mice, prairie dogs and insects, and woe betide any four-footed marauder that is caught foraging there; he is soon roasted and supplying protoplasm to the Moki organism; except in case of a burro, when his ears are docked in proportion to the magnitude or incorrigibility of his misdeed, to brand him publicly as a thief.

BASKET-WEAVER.

MOTHER AND CHILD.

On the rocky side of the mesa are thriving peach orchards, perfectly free from blight or insect enemies, and in the proper season loaded down with luscious fruit of which the Mokis are extravagantly fond. A few cottonwoods among the fields, the peach trees, and the cedars along the mesa sides, are all the trees to be seen. These cedar forests are to the Moki towns what a vein of coal is to a civilized town — the fuel supply always getting farther away and harder to reach, because the annual growth of a desert cedar is almost imperceptible. Though veins of coal peep out in many places near the pueblos, the Mokis do not use it, although they seem to have known what coal is long before our wise men settled the question; the native name for it is "rock wood," *koowa*, a word which resembles our word coal. The score or so of fruits, grains and vegetables which the Mokis plant would, in favorable seasons, cause peace and plenty to reign in Tusayan, but Moki history has some sad tales of famine. When the crops fail, the "good people" of necessity fall back on the crops of nature's own sowing in the desert. Old people still gather a plant for greens, which they say has before now preserved the tribe from starvation. Dried bunches of this plant may often be seen ornamenting the rafters of their dwellings, amidst a medley of other curious things. The fare of the pueblo is eked out in ordinary times with edible roots,

33

SPINNER AND WEAVER.

seeds, berries, and leaves gathered from far and near. The Mokis are practical botanists. No plant has escaped their piercing eyes; they have given them names and found out their good and bad qualities; pressed them into service for food, medicine, religion, basket making and a hundred other uses, from an antidote for snake bites to a hair brush. They are also perforce vegetarians. Oñate, the Conqueror, said slightingly of Zuñi that there were as many rabbits as people around it. Such a condition of things in Tusayan would fill the Moki with joy, for he has the same fondness for rabbit as the negro has for "'possum with coon gravy." Snakes seem to be more plentiful than rabbits, although it takes ardent hunting to catch enough reptiles for the Snake dance. Rats, mice, prairie dogs and an occasional deceased burro or goat vary the menu of the pueblos. The Mokis never eat their dogs, though to do so would be at least putting them to some use.

Centuries ago, when the Mokis lived in the White Mountains and the Mogollones, they must have been hunters. What could have driven them from that paradise of coolness and greenery? There under the giant pines roamed elk, deer, antelope and bear; in the brush were turkey; in the trees birds and squirrels; in the cool streams were trout, and the wild bees furnished delicious honey. There was abundant rain, and in the broad valleys corn could be raised by "dry farming." For

34

PUEBLO OF MISHONGINOVI.

*Hillers, photo.*

PUEBLO OF SHIPAULOVI.

*Hillers, photo.*

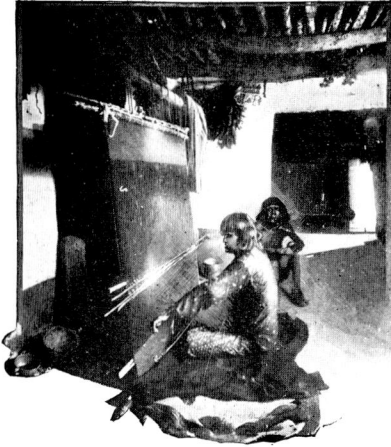

DRESS WEAVING. *Maude, photo.*

that Arizonian oasis of flowers and plenty the ancestors of the M o k i o f t e n must have sighed, but desert and a crust were preferable to the bloodthirsty Apache. This is the history of many an enforced migration.

Now, pursuing the order in which the traveler becomes familiar with the surroundings of the Moki, from the distant approach, when the mesas swim in the mirage with the dim outlines of the cell towns on their crests, to when he encamps by the corn fields and springs at their base, we will next toil up the trail to visit. Far out in the plain the watchful Moki from his high vantage has seen the approach of visitors, and the news flies fast. There will surely be some of the inhabitants to greet the traveler when he arrives, to wonder at his outfit, ask for *piba* and *matchi* (tobacco and matches), run errands and be on the lookout for windfalls of food.

If the traveler wishes a washerman, a boy to graze the horses or carry water and wood, or if he wishes to rent a house, he will soon find willing hands and plenty of advisers. *Shiba* (silver) makes things run smoothly here as in civilization. Starting at the altitude of a mile and one-fourth, the climbing of a mesa

DYER. *Voth, photo.*

is somewhat of a task to the unaccustomed. When the
fierce sun is high, the climb may have frequent periods
of pause, and the natives who run up and down the mesa
as though it were a short flight of stairs are objects
of envy. But when the ascent is made and one sits in
the shade and hospitality of a Moki interior, the exer-
tion is repaid. It is a new and memorable experience.

PUEBLO OF SHUNGOPAVI. *Hillers, photo*

The nineteenth century civilization, with its tall build-
ings and bustling crowds, fades away and we are in the
ancient past of the southwest wonderland.

The Mokis are almost invariably pleased to have
white visitors enter their houses. Most of them invite
you in, all smiles and hospitality. In most cases, though,
where there is any doubt it is better to say, " *een quaqui*

ORAIBI GIRLS GRINDING CORN. *Tipton, photo.*

*ési ?*" (am I welcome?) which brings a hearty response. The houses have thick walls of flat stone, laid up in mud, plastered inside and out, and are pleasantly cool in the summer. The hard, smooth, plastered floor is the general sitting place, with the interposition of a blanket or sheepskin. The low bench, or ledge, which often runs around the room, is also used as a seat. Perhaps the ceiling will appear strange. The large cottonwood beams with smaller cross-poles backed with brush; above that, grass and a top layer of mud form a very picturesque ceiling and effective roof. From the center of the ceiling hangs a feather tied to a cotton string. This is the soul of the house and the sign of its dedication; no house is without one. Around the walls and from the beams hang all sorts of quaint belongings — painted wooden dolls, bows and arrows, strings of dried herbs and mysterious bundles, likely of trappings for the dances—enough to stock a museum. In well-to-do families the blanket pole, extending across the room, is loaded with their riches in the shape of harness, sashes, blankets and various other valuables. In one corner is a fireplace with hood ; sunk in the floor are the corn mills; near by is a large water jar with dipper, and sundry pieces of pottery are scattered about. Usually the

MAKING BREAD (PIKI).

A COURT IN ORAIBI.

*Hillers, photo.*

general assembly room is kept clean with the brushes
made of grass stems, which serve also for hair brushes
betimes. This parlor, sitting room, sleeping room,
dining room and mealing room combined, serves
nearly every purpose of the family; but there is always
a grain room, where the corn is piled in neat rows,
and sometimes a room is set apart for baking. The
houses are rarely higher than two stories, the upper
being set back in terrace style, so that its front door
yard is the roof of the lower. The ladders are picturesque; dogs and chickens, as well as people, climb
up and down. Stone steps on the partition walls
lead to the roofs, and when on top it is possible to
wander almost all over the town, as in the Orient. A jar
with the bottom knocked out caps the chimney, or a
whole stack of jars runs clear up from the lower floor,
securely plastered around the joints, making an excellent chimney. Short billets of piñon or cedar are piled
up on the walls for firewood, and not a chip or strand of
bark is wasted from the family woodpile. From the pro-
jecting beam ends and from pegs in the house front hangs

39

ORAIBI WASHERWOMAN.

an old curiosity shop of articles — eagle traps, gourds, hoes, planting sticks, sheep bones, and many other articles that keep one guessing. On the top of a house in Moki-land once was seen a curi-ous structure, having slanting sides formed of bits of boards. On closer examination it was found to be a plow, which the good people at Washington had sent the Mokis, now doing service as a chicken coop. Outside the door by the street is the *pigame* oven, in which green corn pudding is baked, food dear to the Moki heart and acceptable to any white visitor who does not know that the women chew the yeast to ferment the batter. This oven is a pit in the ground two or three feet deep. Before baking, a fire is made in it, and after the walls of the oven are heated the ashes are raked out and the pudding, called *pigame*, is put in and the top covered with a stone on which the fire is kept burning. The pudding is put in the oven at

PUEBLO OF ORAIBI.

nightfall usually, and by morning
it is well baked and ready to be
wrapped in corn husks for con-
sumption.

A stroll about a Moki town will
convince the explorer that there
are streets full of "surprises," as
we call unexpected nooks and
corners in our own houses. Just
what the building regulations are
no one has yet divulged, but the
lay of the ground has much to do
with the arrangement. Wolpi is
crowded upon the point of a narrow mesa, and some of the houses
are perched on the edge of the
precipice, their foundation walls
going down many feet, the building of which is a piece of adven-
turous engineering. Many of the

SICHOMOVI FOOT TRAIL.

towns have passages under the houses leading from one
street to another. The stone surface of the street is
deeply worn by the bare or moccasined feet of many
generations. The trail over
the dizzy narrows between
Wolpi and Sichomovi is
worn like a wagon track
in places from four to six
inches deep. The end of a
ladder sticking up through
a hatchway in a low mound
slightly above the
level of the street
marks the way
down into an
underground

A MESA CLIFFSIDE.

A MOKI INTERIOR.                    *Vroman, photo.*

room, where strange ceremonies are held. This is a *kiva*,
and if we are hardy enough to brave the usual warning
to the uninitiated, we may peep down without fear of
swelling up and bursting. Perhaps, if there is no ceremony going on, a weaver may be making a blanket
on his simple loom; likely it is deserted, dusky and
quiet with no suggestion of writhing serpents or naked
votaries and weird chanting. All streets lead to the
plaza, the center of interest, set apart for the many
dances; some solemn and awe-inspiring, some grotesque
and amusing; all dramatic in action and marvelous in
color. In the center of the plaza is a stone box. This
is a shrine, the focus at which all ceremonies center, and
beneath it is the opening into the underworld of

POTTERS.

departed ancestors.
Around most plazas in
Tusayan the houses are
built solidly; at Wolpi
the dances take place on
a narrow shelf above
the dizzy sandstone
cliffs; at Oraibi one side of the plaza where the Snake
dance is enacted is open and the distant San Francisco
mountains stand plainly on the horizon.

Outside the town there is also something to see.
The general ash pile with its stray burro engaged in a
hopeless task of finding something to eat is passed by,
and one looks down over the brow of the mesa at the
corrals among the rocks on a narrow ledge crowded with
bleating sheep and goats. The trails wind down the
mesa, across the fields, and are lost in the country lying
spread out below like a map. Under the rocks a woman
is digging out clay for pottery, other women are toiling
up with jars of water from the
springs, while on the steep slope
among the jagged fragments of
stone is perhaps the last resting
place of the inhabitants, strewn
with bits of pottery. The springs
in Tusayan come out near the
base of the mesas, and the labor
of carrying water up some 600 feet
by means of the female beast of
burden puts water at a premium.
It is a blessing that the dry,
searching air of the elevated
region, and the fierce sun, do not
render bathing an actual necessity. Most of the springs yield
little water, so that a large party

43

A MOKI FAMILY.

AN ORAIBI GIRL.

of visitors with horses camping about a pueblo will give rise to fears of a water famine. Placed on the borders of every spring, down close to the water, may be seen short painted sticks with feather plumes — prayer offerings to the gods for a continued supply of the precious fluid, the scarcity of which from clouds or springs has had to do with the origin of many ceremonies in the Southwest. The lack of water even fills in a large part of the conversation of white visitors in this dry country, taking the place of the weather, which is unlikely to change.

Let us follow up the trail again after the toiling water carriers, returning from the general meeting and gossiping place, the spring. Let no one think that there has been a lack of company in the course of these wanderings. There are the children first, last and all the time, all pervading, timid, but made bold by the prospect of sweets. It is amusing to see a little tot come hesitatingly as near as he dares to a white visitor, and say, "Hel-lo ken-te" (candy). Unclad before three or four years of age, the little ones look like animated bronzes — "fried cupids," one amused onlooker has termed them. The older girls have general charge of the young ones, and carry them about pick-a-back; sometimes it is difficult to tell whether the carrier or

44

the carried is the larger. The children are good, and seem never to need correction, and anyone can see with half an eye that the Mokis love their little ones. They never are so flattered as when attention is paid to the children. Do this with an admiring look, accompanied by the word "*Lo'-lomai*" (good, excellent, pretty), and the parental heart is won. When the rains fill the rock basins on the mesa, these youngsters have a famous time bathing, squirming like tadpoles in the pools, splashing and chasing each other. The

A MISHONGINOVI GIRL.

Moki childlife must be a uniformly happy one, except in the season of green things, when they are allowed to eat without limit. The statistics of highest mortality must coincide with the time of watermelons, which are never

too unripe to eat. Dogs, chickens and burros also add to the picturesqueness of a Moki village. The burros have the run of the town, and furnish amusement for the children. When providence or luck has prevented a burro from stealing corn, his ears have a normal, if not graceful length. Few there are, though, that have not paid penalty by the loss of one or both of these appendages. Chickens and dogs are a sorry lot. The latter lie in the corners and shady places, and only become animate and vocal at night, with true coyote instinct.

45

A MISHONGINOVI WOMAN.

SNAKE KIVA, ORAIBI.

A shrill whistle denotes that some Moki is the fortunate possessor of an eagle to supply him with the prized feathers for ceremonials. The man who is opulent enough to keep a turkey also has feathers for the gathering. Women go about on various errands or pay visits in which gossip bears a large share. Many a pair of dark eyes peep out from the light-hole in the walls of the houses, or a maiden with hair done up in whorls takes a modest glance at the strangers. The weird, high-pitched songs of the corn grinders, and the rumble of the mealing-stones, are familiar sounds in a Moki village. If you see a woman or maiden with face powdered with corn flour, it means that she has been busy grinding in the hopper-like mills sunken in the floor of every house,— and very hard labor it is. Most of the able-bodied men are in the fields if the time is summer, that is if no ceremony is going on — a rare contingency. Moki men are not afraid of work. From youth until the time when they are enrolled in the class of the lame, halt and blind, they do their share for the support of the clan. Not averse to soothing the baby as his white brother sometimes may be, his domestic habits will not take him so far as to do women's work. Since the time when his sweetheart combed his raven locks in sign of betrothal, and he

ANTELOPE ALTAR IN KIVA.

had woven the wedding blanket, and the simple marriage forms were observed, the traditional division of labor has not been transgressed. Man's work and woman's work are portioned off by the laws of unalterable custom. The division seems fair as to the amount of labor. A popular illusion that the Indian makes his wife do all the work is dispelled here, as another, that Indians are always gruff and taciturn, will vanish after a quarter of an hour's acquaintance with the jovial, laughing Mokis. The house belongs to the woman, and it is proper that she should do the labor connected with it, grind the corn, carry the water, do the cooking, keep the house tidy, and mind the baby. Fortunately, Moki babies do not long require much attention; they soon take care of themselves under the general supervision of the older children. The young boys, perhaps, with bow in hand, go to the field with the men, for here is where man's work comes in under the broiling sun, preparing the ground, planting the crops, hoeing, keep-

*Vroth, photo*

WOMEN'S DANCE, ORAIBI.

ing off the crows, prairie dogs, mice and insects, setting up breaks against the wind or sudden rush of water, gathering the crops and bringing them to the house on the mesa. He brings wood chopped from the piñons and cedars several miles away, and hustles generally to supply the family. If he has horses and a wagon by the bounty of *Wasintona*, he may get odd jobs of hauling, which bring him in money for sugar, coffee and white

47

THIEF BURRO.

man's flour, purchasable from the trader. Besides their customary work, some of the women have other occupations. At the East Mesa she may be a potter, at the Middle Mesa or Oraibi a basket maker, but never a weaver, for that, strangely enough, is man's work. In the quiet of her house the basket maker is busy, for are not many *Pahanas* coming to the Snake dance? Sugar and baking powder for the feast may depend on the sales of baskets. Around her on the floor are gay colored splints of yucca leaf, dyed with the evanescent aniline colors introduced by the traders. Some of the strips are being moistened in a bed of damp sand, from which they are taken to be sewn through and over, covering the coil of grass with geometric designs. The needle is really an awl; now of iron, formerly of bone. At Oraibi, where one of the three Snake dances held in Tusayan in the even years occurs, painted baskets of wicker are made. They are very decorative. The potter also plies her craft for the advent of the white man. The clay has been gathered, prepared, and made into vessels of forms tempting to the visitor, painted and burned at the foot of the mesa so that the villainous smoke will not choke everyone. Her wares are quaint and not half bad. Nampeo, at Hano, is the best potter in all Moki-land.

Of course little figures have to be carved from cottonwood, painted and garnished to resemble the numerous divinities of the Mokis who take part in the ceremonies. Men and women make them for their children, who thus get kindergarten instruction on the appearance of the inhabitants of the spiritual world. These "dolls" can often be bought; they are among the most curious souvenirs of the Moki. The weaver, too, spends his odd times in weaving the far-famed blankets of wool, dyed blue with sunflower seeds. He knows well the way to weave pretty diaper patterns which remind one of French worsted designs. The blankets are serviceable to the last degree and in the loose garment of the women will, perhaps, endure a whole generation. Belts of bright colored yarns, embroidered kilts of cotton and embroidered woolen sashes are *chef-d'œuvres* of the weaver.

The light side of life is uppermost in Moki-land. The disposition of the Moki is to make work a sport, necessity a pleasure and to have a laugh or joke ready in an instant. This is the home of song makers; the singing of the men at work, of the mother to her babe, of the corn grinders, of the priests in assembly chamber or in the *kiva*-vault, constantly ripples forth. There is no need for songs of the day; love songs, lullabys, war songs, hunting songs, songs secular and religious give variety in plenty. The dark side exists, to be sure, but the Mokis are so like children that a smile lurks just behind a sorrow. The seriousness and gravity with which the ceremonials are conducted is very impressive, and no one who has seen the Snake dance will fail to note that the Moki can be grave at times. Telling stories is one of the amusements of winter around the fireside. Until the ground is frozen it is dangerous to relate the deeds of the ancients : then they have gone away and will not overhear to the harm of the story-teller. Rabbit hunting is another favorite amusement, and parties of young men often do more hard work in one day thus than in a month otherwise with few results to show of "long ears" slain by the curved boomerang. In the proper season berrying parties go out for a day's picnic; the Mokis enjoy traveling, and a journey of fifteen or twenty miles to a berry patch and back is not thought anything out of common. When the green corn comes then the Moki lives bountifully. Tall columns of white steam arising in the cornfields at early morning invite to a feast of roast corn taken from the newly opened pit-oven. Then there is feasting while the ears are hot and jollity reigns. One thing will strike the visitor as curious : the Mokis do not gamble or drink fire-water, even when they have an opportunity. They do like tobacco, though, and the visitor who smokes will do well to lay in an extra supply, for after the first greeting, "*piti*," the next query will be "*piba*" (tobacco), followed by "*matchi*" (matches), and a friendly smoke council is held then and there.

The Mokis are the best entertained people in the world. A round of ceremonies, each terminating in the pageants called "dances," keeps going pretty continuously the whole year. The theaters and other shows in the closely built pueblos of the white man fall far short of entertaining all the people, as do the Moki shows. Then the Moki spectacles are free. The scheme of having a gatekeeper on the trails to demand an entrance fee, while it has great possibilities, has never entered the Moki mind. This, too, for a good reason. These ceremonies are religious and make up the complicated worship of the people of Tusayan. Even a visitor bent on sightseeing alone will be impressed with the seriousness of the Indian dancers and the evidence of deep feeling — perhaps it should be called devotion — in the onlookers. Not only in the somber Snake dance, but in every other ceremony of Tusayan the actors are inspired by one purpose and that is to persuade the gods to give rain and abundant crops. So the birds that fly, the reptiles that creep, are made messengers to the great nature gods with petitions, and the different ancestors and people in the underworld are notified that the ceremony is going on that they too may give their aid. The amount of detail connected with the observance of one of the ceremonies is almost beyond belief, and being carried on in the dark *kivas* has rarely been witnessed by others

than the initiated priests. Thus the
many observances which come around
from time to time in two years are
quite a tax on the memory of the
adepts.

The ceremonial year of the Moki
is divided equally by two great events,
the departure of the *kachinas* in
August and their arrival in Decem-
ber. The *kachinas* are the spirits of
the ancestors whose special pleasure
it is to watch over Tusayan. When
the crops are assured they depart for

A TEWA GIRL.

*Nuvatikiobi,* "the place of the high snows," or San
Francisco Mountain. After their departure come the
Snake and Flute dances, among others, and all the
dances up to the return of the *kachinas* are called
"nine days' ceremonies," while the joyous *kachina*
dances are known as the "masked dances."

All who become acquainted with the Mokis learn to
respect and like them. Fortunate is the person who,
before it is too late, sees under so favorable aspect their
charming life in the old new world.

WALTER HOUGH.

## THE SNAKE LEGEND.

The Snake dance is an elaborate prayer for rain, in which the
reptiles are gathered from the fields, intrusted with the prayers of
the people, and then given their liberty to bear these petitions to
the divinities who can bring the blessing of copious rains to the
parched and arid farms of the Hopis. It is also a dramatization of
an ancient half-mythic, half-historic legend dealing with the origin
and migration of the two fraternities which celebrate it, and by
transmission through unnumbered generations of priests has become conventionalized to a degree, and possibly the actors themselves could not now explain the significance of every detail of the
ritual. The story is of an ancestral Snake-youth, Ti'yo, who, pon-
dering the fact that the water of the river flowed ever in the same

direction past his home without returning or filling up the gorge below, adventurously set out to ascertain what became of it. He carried with him, by paternal gift, a precious box containing some eagle's down and a variety of prayer-sticks (pahos) for presentation to the Spider-woman, the Ancient of the Six Cardinal Points, the Woman of the Hard Substance (such as turquoise, coral and shell), the Sun, and the underworld divinity who makes all the germs of life. The Spider-woman was propitiated and cordially became his counselor and guide. She prepared a liquid charm to be taken in the mouth and spurted upon angry beasts and snakes for their pacification, and perched herself invisibly on his ear. Then through the *sipapu* they plunged to the underworld. There, following floating wisps of the eagle's down, they journeyed from place to place, safely passing the great snake Gato'ya, and savage wild beast sentinels, visiting Hi'canavaiya, who determines the path of the rain-clouds, and Hi'zriingwikti, the ancient woman who every night becomes an enchanting maiden ; had a smoke with Ta'wa, the Sun, and went with him to inspect the place where he rises ; meeting Müiyingwuh on the way and receiving friendly assurances from that creative divinity. He rode across the sky on the Sun's shoulder and saw the whole world, and learned from his flaming charioteer that the possession most dearly to be prized was the rain-cloud. So he returned to the kiva near the great snake, and from the Snake Antelope men there learned what songs to sing, what prayer-sticks to fashion and how to paint his body, that the rain-cloud might come. The chief gave him much important paraphernalia, and two maidens who knew the charm preventing death from the bite of the rattlesnake. These maidens Tiyo took home, giving one to his younger brother, where the youthful couples took up their abode in separate kivas. At night low clouds trailed over the village, and Snake people from the underworld came from them and went into the kivas. On the following morning they were found in the valleys, transformed into reptiles of all kinds. This occurred for four days. Then (ninth morning) the Snake maidens said, " We understand this ; let the younger brothers (the Snake Society) go out and bring them all in and wash their heads, and let them dance with you." This was done, and prayer-meal sprinkled upon them, and then they were carried back to the valleys, and they returned to the Snake kiva of the underworld bearing the petitions of all the people.

(Condensed from the account by J. Walter Fewkes, in Jour. Am. Ethn. and Arch., Vol. IV.)

It is only the ninth day's ceremony, the dance with the snakes, which is publicly performed.

# MOKI CEREMONIES.

It will be noted that the Snake dances occur during the month of August, the date being between the 15th and 26th, and announced a few days prior to the beginning of the nine days' ceremonies, of which the dance is the public culmination. In the even years (1902, 1904, 1906, etc.) they occur at Oraibi, Shipaulovi and Sichomovi; in the odd years (1901, 1903, 1905, etc.), at Wolpi and Mishonginovi. The Flute dances, a picturesquely impressive but less exciting ceremony, occur at the above-named pueblos in years alternating with the Snake dance. For example, 1900 being the year of the Snake dance at Oraibi, the Flute dance at that pueblo will occur in 1901; and 1899 having been the year of the Snake dance at Wolpi, a Flute dance occurred there in 1900.

## ROUTES TO THE MOKI PUEBLOS.

Far from being difficult of access, the Province of Tusayan is easily reached either by saddle horse or wheel conveyance from several towns on the Santa Fe Pacific Railroad, a division of the transcontinental line of the Santa Fe route. The trip can be made most conveniently by travelers to or from California as a side excursion *en route*, but the experience will amply repay a special journey across the continent. Some fatigue and lack of comforts incident to roughing it are well-nigh inseparable from such an excursion, involving as it does the traversing of from seventy to over one hundred miles of the Great American Desert, depending upon the point selected for departure from the railroad. But these very features are accounted no small part of the attractions of the trip, as lovers of outdoor life amid scenes of novel and extraordinary interest need not be told. Indeed, if the pueblos as an objective point did not exist, a voyage into that country of extinct volcanoes and strangely sculptured and tinted rocks and mesas would be well worth the making. While the round trip from the railroad may be made in four or five days, or less if desired, it can be pleasurably prolonged indefinitely. Aside from the powerful charm exerted by this region upon all visitors, there is an invigorating tonic quality in the pure air of Arizona that is better than medicine for the overworked in the exhausting activities of city business life. Many a professional man (and woman), wearied in brain and enfeebled in body, having been solicited to make this or a similar outdoor excursion in Arizona, has complied with misgiving and returned almost miraculously restored to health and vigor. Testimony to this fact can be furnished by reference to many well-known individuals, who, were they entirely free to indulge their preferences, would every summer forego the seaside and the fashionable watering-place and return to Arizona to mount a sturdy bronco, and forget for a time the cares and conventionalities of civilized life in a simple, wholesome and joyous existence in the sunlit air of the desert.

At the stations named all needful transportation facilities are provided, whose proprietors are accustomed to convey passengers every summer to the Snake dances. A visit to the Moki pueblos may, however, be made at any season, except in midwinter, and will at any time prove richly interesting. Arrangements should be made in advance by correspondence, which may be addressed to either the local agent of the Santa Fe, W. J. Black, General Passenger Agent, Topeka, Kan., or Chicago; W. S. Keenan, General Passenger Agent, Galveston; Jno. J. Byrne, General Passenger Agent, Los Angeles; or John L. Truslow, General Agent, San Francisco.

[NOTE. — The distances given are approximate, as in some cases, particularly between the different pueblos, they depend upon whether the wagon or the horse trail is followed, the latter being shorter. The transportation charges also depend somewhat upon the size of the party. One or two persons traveling light by way of the shortest route could reach Oraibi in one day if desired. Larger or more leisurely parties would require two days, or longer by the less direct routes.]

## Cañon Diablo Route.

| | | |
|---|---|---|
| To McAllister's Crossing .................... | 15 | miles |
| Volz's Store, "The Fields" ............. | 17 | " |
| Little Burro Spring ..................... | 22 | " |
| Big Burro Spring ....................... | 3 | " |
| Oraibi................................. | 16 | " |
| | 73 | " |
| Middle Mesa ........................... | 20 | " |
| | 93 | " |
| Wolpi ...................... ............ | 10 | " |
| | 103 | " |

NOTE.— From "The Fields" there is a horse trail, northeasterly course, to Middle Mesa, 43 miles, and to Wolpi, 53 miles.

CHARGES.—$20 round trip, for conveyance by wagon ; meals $1 each, and lodging $1 per night.

## Winslow Route.

### 1.

| | | |
|---|---|---|
| To Rocky Ford Crossing .......... | 9 miles | |
| Junction with Cañon Diablo road north of Volz's Store........ | 30 " | |
| Little Burro.................... | 20 " | |
| | | 59 miles |
| Oraibi........................ | 20 " | |
| | 79 " | |
| Wolpi ................................. | 22 " | |
| | 81 " | |
| Wolpi to Middle Mesa...................... | 10 " | |
| Middle Mesa to Oraibi ..................... | 20 " | |
| | 111 " | |

### 2.

| | | |
|---|---|---|
| To Rocky Ford Crossing.................... | 9 miles | |
| Pyramid Butte......................... | 26 " | |
| Commoh's Spring...................... | 10 " | |
| Touchez-de-nez (Sigenis) ............... | 25 " | |
| Wolpi ................................. | 5 " | |
| | 75 | |
| Middle Mesa........................... | 10 " | |
| Oraibi .............................. | 20 " | |
| | 105 | |

CHARGES.— Named on application. Team and driver for four should cost not to exceed $5 per day, passengers furnishing their own bedding and provisions. Winslow is provided with hotel accommodations and outfitting stores.

## Holbrook Route.

To La Reaux Wash .......................... 11 miles
    Well near Cottonwood Wash............. 6   "
    Cottonwood Wash crossing .......... ... 3   "
    Malpais Spring.......................... 13  "
    Bittahoochee........................... 7   "
    Tonnael Malpais Spring ................ 12  "
    Jeditoh Valley Spring................... 22  "
    Keam's Cañon .......................... 6   "
    Wolpi ................................. 10  "

                                       90  "
    Middle Mesa........................... 10  "
    Oraibi ................................ 20  "

                                     120  "

CHARGES.— $15 round trip, for conveyance by wagon, passengers providing their own camp outfit and provisions. Holbrook has good livery and hotel accommodations, and stores.

## Flagstaff Route.

To Turkey Tanks ....................... .... 19 miles
    Grand Falls Crossing.................... 22 "
    Little Burro............................ 45 "
    Oraibi ................................ 18 "
                                         —
                                           104 "

    Middle Mesa........................... 20 "
    Wolpi ................................ 10 "
                                           —
                                         134 "

CHARGES.— For wagon conveyance, $25 round trip. Board $3 per day, and lodging $1 per night. Or passengers may provide their own outfit and provisions and arrange with liverymen for transportation only. Hotel accommodations, livery and stores at Flagstaff are excellent.

It is also practicable to make the trip from Gallup. This route is not shown on map herein, but is reported to be as below :

To Rock Spring Store ..................... 9 miles
    Hay Stack Store ....................... 12 "
        (Fort Defiance, 9 miles north.)
    Cienega................................ 5 "
    Bear Tank (water 1½ miles north)........ 20 "
    Cotton & Hubbell's Store (Gañada) ...... 11 "
    Eagle Crag (water 1½ miles north)....... 23 "
    Steamboat Cañon (water 3 miles north)... 8 "
    Keam's Cañon School .................. 18 "
    Keam's Cañon Store.................... 2 "
    Wolpi ................................ 10 "
                                           —
                                         118 "

    Middle Mesa.................. ......... 10 "
    Oraibi ................................ 20 "
                                           —
CHARGES.—Named on application.   148 "

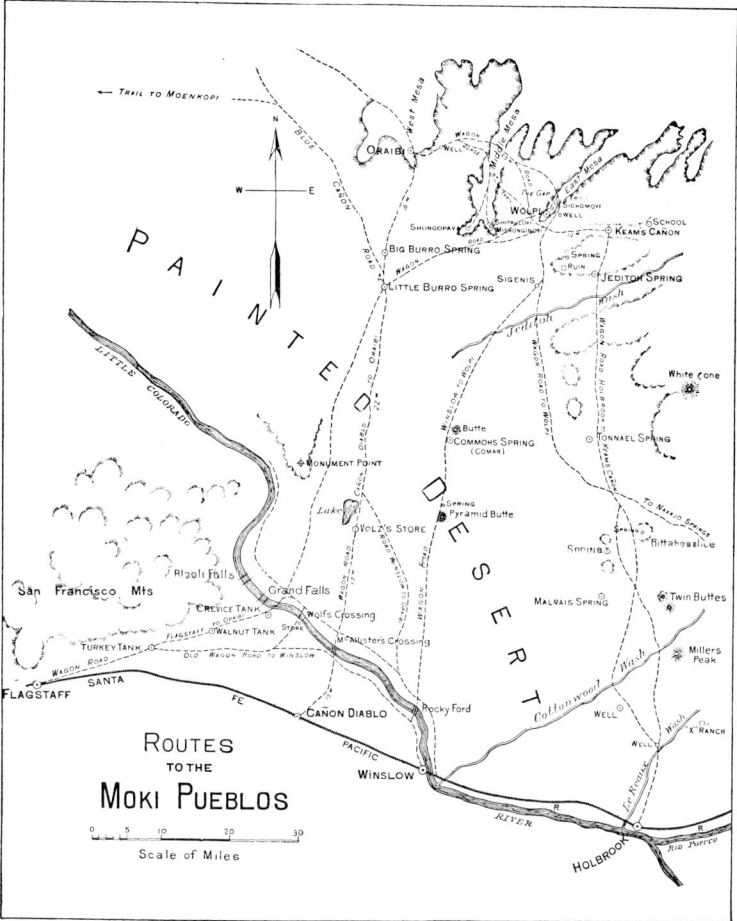

ROUTES
TO THE
MOKI PUEBLOS

Scale of Miles

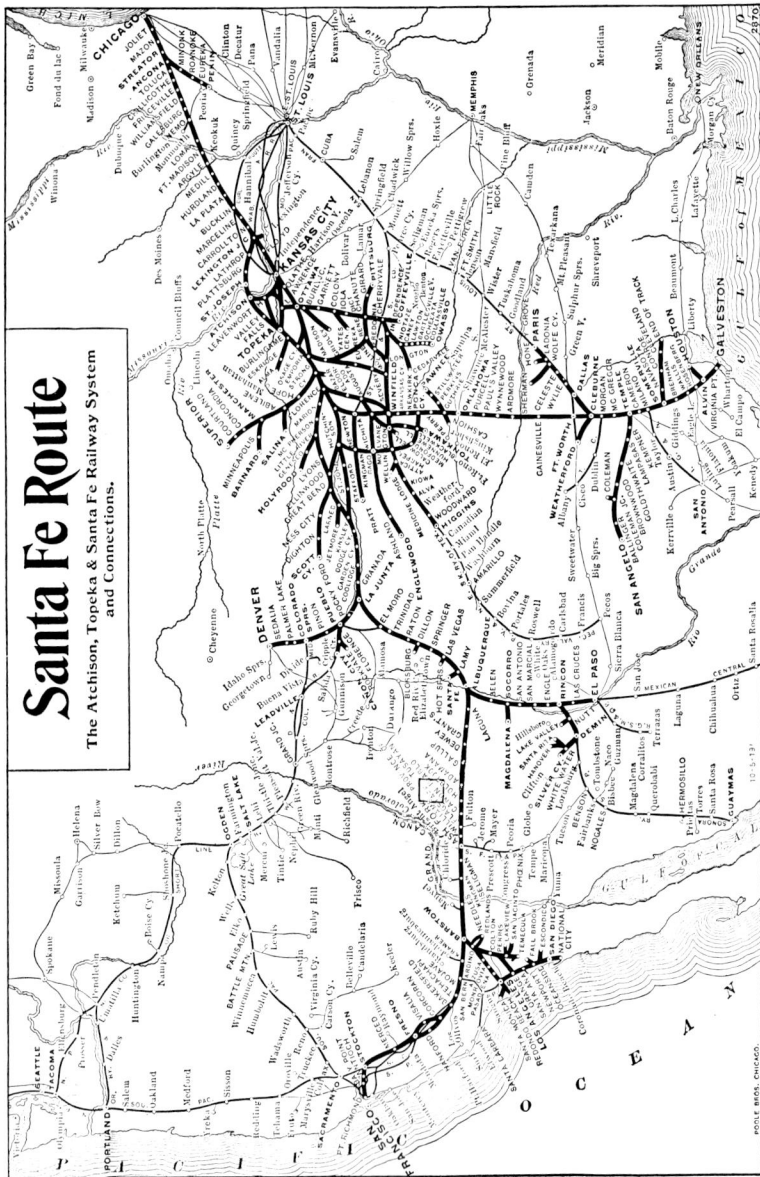

# Santa Fe Route

The Atchison, Topeka & Santa Fe Railway System and Connections.

The Province of Tusayan, site of the Moki Pueblos, is situated north of the railroad west of Albuquerque, and is thus indicated : ☐

THE·HENRY·
O·SHEPARD·
CO.

CHICAGO

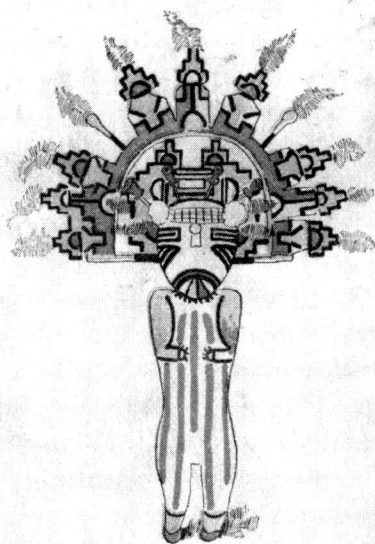